Cryptocurrency:

Donate Coins for Massive Gains

CHRISTOPHER JACOBS

Table of Contents

Introduction

I would like to thank you for purchasing this book: "Cryptocurrency: Donate Coins for Massive Gains" which can be considered as a simple guide to understand the cryptocurrency market and the different ways to secure the crypto coins without losing them to high taxes.

The primary purpose of the book is to take you through cryptocurrency regulation, helping to understand the HODL concept, the different types of taxes that can be levied on the crypto users during cryptocurrency transactions, the purpose of donating crypto coins and the benefits it can provide.

In 2017, a majority of people had come forward to know more and understand better about the digital currency compared to the previous years. Many corporate companies, financial institutions, and banks had made elaborate attempts to research on "Cryptocurrency" and the monetary benefits it can bring to their respective economic setup. Many cryptocurrencies, especially Bitcoin, had seen a steep rise and fall in its value but the overall output was beneficial to the investors and traders who had chosen to try their luck with the said digital currency. 2018 is expected to see newer crypto investors' in the digital market who will be trying to make the best out of the crypto coins.

Financial experts started looking at the digital currency as a form of investment to make quick money though it is still considered to be volatile with high-risk factors. Bitcoins, Ethereum and Litecoins – the popular cryptocurrencies in the market have seen a steady rise in having more investors and traders who were keen to make financial benefits using these digital coins.

In this book, we will be discussing more about cryptocurrency, the role of tax on the said digital currency and the advantages it holds in donating coins for better gains. The chapters will give readers more detailing on the HODL concept, the possibility of tax inclusion and benefits of donating the crypto coins.

I hope this book will help you by detailing out the benefits of donating crypto coins in the cryptocurrency market. There are a good number of charitable trusts and non-profit organizations that have increased their donor base because of cryptocurrencies. I hope this book serves as an informative and exciting read for you!

Happy reading!

Chapter One: Regulating Cryptocurrencies

Cryptocurrency is not only looked at as a 'digital currency' but has also been sure to make its presence felt in the economic market as a smart and prospective way to be a promising investment asset. Though it is highly volatile and risky, crypto coins have already made a mark in the digital market, which has attracted a lot of investors and traders. Since 2009, Bitcoin has not only become the most popular cryptocurrency in the financial market but is still considered to be one of the oldest cryptocurrencies in the crypto world. The confidence among the investors has become high since the remarkable increase in the Bitcoin value for over a year now.

Even though there is still confusion on how to buy a cryptocurrency; the economic market has not failed to show a considerable increase in the number of people who have purchased the coins, invested in them or made money by trading them with other crypto coins. It is possible to make money by buying or selling cryptocurrencies, trading two different cryptocurrencies or by converting wealth (assets) from Bitcoin or other crypto coins to 'fiat currencies' and vice-versa. When the regulatory bodies understood that there is quite an amount of money flow using this virtual currency, they wanted to regulate the flow of these digital coins by imposing taxation on the virtual money.

According to the IRS (Internal Revenue Service), cryptocurrency is no longer considered as a currency, but it is referred as 'personal property' thereby making it taxable. To be more specific, the income generated from the sale of cryptocurrencies is subject to either short-term or long-term taxations for the investors or traders. In the case of retirement account investors, the taxation process is favorable to them. No tax is levied for the retirement account investors, but if the person is interested in mining Bitcoins, then he will fall under the tax category as mining is considered as a source of business income.

If the asset (crypto coins) is held for short-term (less than twelve months), the investor or trader will be subject to ordinary income tax rates. If the asset (crypto coins) is held for long-term (more than twelve months), he or she will be subject to 15% - 20% based on the income value. The period and the tax value can differ based on the currency value and tax laws in various countries.

Cryptocurrency Taxation

Many countries are looking to regulate cryptocurrencies by defining them as either of the following:

- Commodity
- Assets
- Asset value
- Property

These digital currencies are not treated as technical currencies, but can still be traded with other cryptocurrencies, goods or services and can also be exchanged for the fiat currencies like INR, USD, EUR, etc. To keep track of all the monetary flows happening among the investors and traders, the regulators are trying to take control by forcing regulations on these digital currencies and overseeing the transaction in a detailed manner. Anyone who is engaged in cryptocurrency transactions will automatically be subjected to general tax or income tax based on his or her respective country's tax policies. Tax regulators in most countries define cryptocurrencies as "property" gained from capital investment(s) or income through cryptocurrency trading (Bitcoin trading, mostly).

Different countries and their take on cryptocurrency regulation

In Germany, 'mining' is considered as a business and the person who 'mines' the cryptocurrency will be subjected to pay 'company tax.' Holding Bitcoins for more than a year will not be subjected to capital gains tax. If any cryptocurrency is received as a source of income, then it will be subjected to income tax.

In Australia, cryptocurrencies are exempt from goods-and-services tax (GST).

In Japan, Bitcoin is looked at as 'asset-like value' and is officially recognized as a 'mode of payment.' As of 1ˢᵗ July 2017, the consumption tax is exempted if Bitcoins are sold. If one gains profit using crypto trading (Bitcoin), he or she will need to pay income tax, company tax or capital gains tax based on the income rate.

In the European Union (EU), cryptocurrency is termed as 'foreign currency.'

UK, Germany, and Switzerland have exempted VAT fees for cryptocurrency transactions.

If the taxpayers are holding on to their crypto investments, they get subjected to capital gains tax between the range of 0% to 25% in countries like Canada, Brazil, Australia, Germany, the US and the UK.

The majority of the countries treat profits gained from crypto trading as a source of 'business income,' and by default, they are applicable to pay capital tax, income tax or company tax based on the income rate.

What led to taxation on cryptocurrencies?

Most of the cryptocurrency investors have been quoting the "like-kind" tax code exemption to avoid paying taxes on cryptocurrency exchanges. This exemption was allowed for property exchange with no tax event creation. Since cryptocurrency was not declared as taxable property then, the crypto traders used to exchange creative works (arts) and properties (real estate) without having to pay taxes on the transactions. Many such transactions happened under the 'like-kind' tax code benefitting traders to make huge money without the need to pay taxes for the crypto exchanges or the transactions made. This resulted in the IRS releasing a statement that cryptocurrency will no longer be considered as currency, but as "property." Since cryptocurrencies were declared as "property," the financial advisors and lawyers have interpreted that cryptocurrency can be exchanged with another cryptocurrency without the need to pay tax on the transaction because, as per the "like-kind" code, two properties can be traded or exchanged with tax exemption. However, cryptocurrency investors were subjected to capital gains tax according to the IRS when they exchanged one crypto coin with another crypto coin as they had "attained a capital gain or monetary gain" during the transaction.

Coinbase, the popular cryptocurrency exchange, was forced to hand over the records of all the investors from 2013 to 2015 when many cryptocurrency investors failed to file their tax returns and published the loss-gain made through cryptocurrency investments for those years. After this episode, the virtual currency was scrutinized entirely, and steps were taken to regulate all the crypto transactions.

When an investor or trader has a majority of his investments in the cryptocurrency domain, he will need to pay income taxes, capital gain taxes, high transaction fees, etc. as the value of cryptocurrency keeps showing considerable increase as days pass by. The IRS is spending more resources on technology to track the cryptocurrency users and Bitcoin users, the crypto world might respond to this with more complicated technology -'cryptography.'

Tax on Bitcoins

Based on the frequency of the transaction, the Bitcoin investor or trader will be subjected to taxation. Let us look at the ways Bitcoin transactions would be treated as a mode of income:

- Business income (Gains arising from Bitcoins because of trading)
- Source income (Increase in prices when the Bitcoin is held as an investment, and then a trade is made)
- Business income and business loss (Regular buying and selling of Bitcoins – 'gains = business income' and 'loss = business loss')
- Capital assets (Bitcoins bought for investment purposes)

When profit is made by selling a Bitcoin, which is held for a longer duration, the investor will have to pay capital gains tax. Short-term capital gains (holding Bitcoins less than 36 months) will be taxable as per the normal tax slabs based on your country's tax regulations and long-term capital gains (holding Bitcoins more than 36 months) will be taxed at maximum 20% of income value.

What is HODL?

HODL was a typo error made by an investor in one of the blog forums when he was mentioning that he had been 'holding' on to his cryptocurrency even after the serious fall that happened in BTC (Bitcoin). The term later became popular among the crypto investors in the digital market as 'hodling' or 'hodl.' It now has a witty backronym –

"**H**old **O**n for **D**ear **L**ife'.

The word 'hodl' means – "hold on to the cryptocurrency even when the value is low and keep a cool head." When you look at Bitcoin as a long-term cryptocurrency, you will not panic about the price going down drastically and will definitely take measures to hold on to it; as you know that there are high chances of getting good profits with the BTC value getting high within a specific period. When the right time comes, you can then comfortably trade the BTC for other altcoins or sell them for a reasonable amount.

Why should you hodl Bitcoin or other crypto coins?

2017 witnessed a 73.3% increase in the value of Bitcoin on one particular week in the month of December. Though there was a considerable decrease in the Bitcoin value, the average growth on the BTC value had been more compared to the decrease in value. People who had held on to their Bitcoins in 2010 are now multi-millionaires as this cryptocurrency has seen an increase of 583170000% from its value in May 2010. It is the fact that "Bitcoins cannot be mined beyond a particular number due to its complex algorithm protocol" which by default will increase its demand to many folds in the near future. Though the virtual currency is highly volatile, it is always wise to hodl (hold) onto the crypto coins for at least a year before trading or selling.

The US gives incentive to Bitcoin holders if they hodl on to their BTC for more than a year to gain long-term capital gains and will be taxed at a much lower rate. The hyperinflation in the country is reducing the dollar value, and even if the government tries to impose on Bitcoin profits, the cost will be considerably low. Because of the risk involved in cryptocurrencies and Bitcoins, it is always advisable to "not put more money in than the amount you can afford to lose."

If you will want to avoid paying too much of money as a tax on your cryptocurrency transactions, consider "hodling" or "donating" as an option.

Chapter Two: HODLing Cryptocurrencies

HODLing or holding cryptocurrencies helps the crypto investors or traders to gain more benefits in terms of gains or price value. When you hold on to your Bitcoins or crypto coins for a more extended period (more than a year), you get the opportunity of looking at the ups and downs of that particular crypto coin's value for a considerably extended period. You will also get an option of analyzing the average increase in the price value and get a fair idea of what benefits you are about to experience for holding the crypto coins on a long-term basis. Based on the supply and demand, the price value of the cryptocurrencies keeps fluctuating dangerously, but even after all these; the market for these virtual coins doesn't seem to go down.

Is there a dilemma?

Bitcoin saw a plunge close to 30% in its price value during the week before Christmas in 2017, which continued to keep rising and falling almost on hourly, daily and monthly basis. The majority of the crypto investment population started chanting the mantra to HODL – Hang or Hold on for dear life. This, indeed, did raise alarm bells to a few investors and they coined a new term – GTHO or **G**et **T**he **H**ell **O**ut.

But more people held on to their HODL chants and started to open up on social networking sites such as Twitter and other chat forums that it is better to HODL than to GTHO since the crypto coin is more of a revolution due to the unique technology (blockchain technology) it runs on. To understand the value of Bitcoin for long-term benefits, daily price fluctuations shouldn't make any difference as when you look at all the historical transactions since 2009, almost the majority of the price dip had only helped in amplifying the price value of the Bitcoins or crypto coins.

Limiting a specific value of capital, which you are not afraid to lose and investing them on to crypto coins should be a smart investor's strategy. Instead of getting anxious every time the crypto coins encounter a decrease in price value, it is sensible to keep your cool by 'holding on to your crypto coins' and waiting for the right time. But if you are very sensitive and cannot bear to keep hearing your heartbeat drumming in your ear every time there is a decrease in the price value, then it is better 'not to get in.' You don't need to end up in a loss by switching on the panic mode and selling the crypto coins at the wrong time.

"Don't put all your apples in one basket" – Haven't we all heard this quote? Well, it is applicable for the crypto investors or traders too.

Instead of putting your focus entirely on one particular crypto coin, have a diversified alternative. It is always better to have a profit gain through one door when you just encountered a loss through another door. Don't hesitate to take advantage of the new cryptocurrency economy by HODLing – working to hold the crypto coins for long-term investment without 'giving in' to the 'temptation to sell' is the best possible way to make gains.

Many crypto investors have claimed to make money by HODLing the crypto coins than by 'trading' them.

Are there any risks involved in HODLing?

Holding crypto coins does involve some risk factor because of which most advisors in the investment field keep repeating the following mantra:

"Never invest more than you can afford to lose."

Let us make a simple and more straightforward comparison to understand the possibilities of the risk involved in holding crypto coins.

"Assume you have deposited the gold you own in a safety locker box in your bank and you have been given the locker's key. You are very confident that your gold is safe in the bank because of the strong high bank walls, heavy iron vaults, complex locker codes and strict security measures taken by the bank. Now all you need to do is keep that locker's key safe. What would happen if the security of the bank is breached and compromised? Before you even realize what had happened, you would end up losing all the gold you had locked up in that secured large iron vault. The matter gets worse when you know the gold lost cannot be recovered by any chance. Now imagine the same thing happening to the cryptocurrencies you have been holding onto in crypto exchanges or online wallets."

Yes! It is such a scary thought, and we are going to discuss how to avoid such risks while holding the crypto coins. We will be debating this entirely based on 'custodial perspective.' Are you still confused? Let us try to understand this by comparing traditional methods with crypto methods.

What would be your custodial options when you have 1000 US dollars in hand? How would you want to keep it safe? You can safeguard the money by following any of the below-mentioned options:

- Managing the cash on your own (Having the cash in your physical wallet or keeping it safe at the safety locker of the cupboard in your room.)
- Trying the banking option (Depositing the amount in your savings account)
- Trusting a friend (Entrusting the money to your friend to hold it on your behalf)
- Getting help from a brokerage firm (Approach a brokerage account to trade with cash or hold on to it on your behalf)
- Using a Mobile wallet for safekeeping (Transferring the cash to your PayPal account)

Now let us look at the crypto options for the above traditional options.

Managing the crypto coins on your own

It gets interesting when you handle the custody of crypto coins all by yourself. This can be done because of the distributed database structure (blockchain technology) the cryptocurrencies are made up of. The crypto space offers many varieties of wallets, which can be chosen to hold the crypto coins. These wallets are interfaces that will allow you to interact with the respective blockchain based on your transaction using their individual private key and seed. There are various wallets available such as hardware wallets, paper wallets, full client storage, and thin client storage and web wallets.

Hardware wallets are similar to dongles that can be plugged into the computer. This device allows you to sign in and access the cryptocurrency transactions. Without this physical dongle-like device, it is impossible to send the crypto coins from the hardware wallets and make any purchases. Trezor and Ledger Nano S are two popular secure hardware wallets in the crypto market.

Paper wallets help by running a website offline and generating a private key for the cryptocurrency. This private key is then printed and stored safe (physically) in a vault or in your room. These types of wallets can be used by services that allow you to import your private keys.

Investors or traders rarely use full client storage implementation, as it requires downloading and running the entire Bitcoin blockchain on your local computer for which the system should be connected to the Internet and synced with the blockchain network. This will need maintenance of the custody of all the private keys run on your wallet. This is a tedious process and will eat up a lot of space on your computer.

Thin client storage implementation allows you to run the blockchain locally by maintaining only the 'headers' of all the blockchain transactions made. This will reduce the space taken on the computer as compared to the full client storage. This will enable you to be in order with what is happening in the network and at the same time maintain the private keys to access your wallet.

Web wallets are provided by Blockchain.info (for Bitcoin), MyEtherWallet (for Ethereum) to view your wallet status and send crypto transactions. The access to your web wallet will only be possible when you provide your private key.

Bank-type option for crypto coins

There are not many traditional bank-like setups for crypto banking. BankEx (decentralized banking system, focusing on proof of assets) and OmiseGO (for financial transactions and settlement services) are the crypto banks (not the actual bank), which can help you in securing your crypto coins, though you cannot compare them to traditional banks on the whole.

Trusting a friend with crypto coins

This can be done by giving your hard-earned fiat currency (dollar, rupee, etc.) to your friend and requesting them to invest on cryptocurrencies on your behalf or entrust your crypto to your friend. But this is even riskier unless you have complete trust in your friend because the crypto coins your friend bought with your money is technically your friend's crypto until the moment it is transferred to you.

Getting brokerage help for your crypto

Coinbase is a popular cryptocurrency exchange that provides services similar to traditional brokerage firms. When the crypto coins are held in cryptocurrency exchanges, the exchange actually owns (controls) your crypto coins though they provide access to login to your crypto exchanges to check your exchange wallet or track the transaction details. There is also a possibility of your login credentials to be compromised similarly to the hackings that happen in bank account networks. So it is always advisable to store your crypto coins in hardware wallets or paper wallets rather than trusting them in online exchange wallets. Though two-factor authentications are implemented, it is still advisable to choose offline wallets over online wallets to reduce the risk factor to the minimum.

Mobile wallets for crypto coins

Like PayPal, there are quite a number of mobile wallets available for storing and transacting your crypto coins. Electrum and Jaxx are mobile wallets open online. If you are using an android phone and have gained root access on the Android operating system, it is advisable to disable rooting to get rid of hackers. Or it would be a better idea to take your crypto coins from these mobile wallets.

Things to remember while 'hodling' Bitcoins or any form of cryptocurrencies

As the value of cryptocurrencies keeps growing every day, it is essential and necessary to store your crypto coins in a secured manner. Safeguarding the crypto coins is very important when you have decided to 'hodl' them.

A few things to keep in mind would be:

Lock and hold

Keep refreshing and re-evaluating your security measures concerning cryptocurrencies once in a fortnight or on a monthly basis. Lock your crypto coins in a secure wallet for which you hold the private key. Never store your cryptocurrencies in an exchange wallet for a more extended period. When you carry your crypto coins in wallets like hardware wallets or paper wallets, it feels more secure, and you hold the complete responsibility in case something happens to your coins. Hold your crypto coins for yourself and stop bragging about the amount of BTCs or ETHs you have.

Be smart in choosing your wallet

The two primary ways of storing your cryptocurrencies are through:

- Wallets which allow you to hold your own primary key
- Online wallets where the crypto exchange holds the primary key on your behalf

Your crypto coins will be safe in hardware or paper wallets even if you break the hardware wallet or delete the app by mistake provided you note down your private key and the seed in a book or a word document and save it.

Online wallets such as LocalBitcoins, which is an exchange wallet, will be convenient for traders who keep buying and selling Bitcoins on a regular basis. There have been instances in the past where crypto exchange wallets get hacked, or the online exchange system collapses. This poses a safety threat and it cannot be assured that it will not happen again.

Unique, strong passwords

Always use strong and unique passwords for all your online transactions. Keep changing your password every month and don't use predictable password combinations. Hackers are ingenious in cracking the password codes if they are too simple with combinations that can be easily predicted. If you feel that you have a feeble memory when it comes to recalling new or complex passwords, use password manager apps.

Double the authentication process

Enable two-factor authentications on all your crypto transactions – be it your email account or exchange account linked to your cryptocurrency wallets. Bitfinex (cryptocurrency exchange) force their customers to enable and activate their two-factor authentication. Many such crypto exchanges are pushing their users to activate the 2FA (Two-factor authentication). Instead of using SMS verification or on-call verification code, choose 2FA hardware key or Google Authenticator to secure your accounts. The cyber attackers are smart enough to trick the customer service staff into porting a mobile number to a new handset (transferring the number to a different network) and use it to bypass the 2FA.

Stop clicking links sent to email IDs or messengers

Don't commit the mistake of clicking on a link or downloading an attachment that claims to be from the crypto wallet providers. Most of these are phishing attacks or scammers. By clicking the links or downloading the attachment, you end up in a high-risk situation where there are chances of your crypto account getting compromised.

More smart tips

- Don't use public Wi-Fi networks to log in to your Bitcoin or crypto wallet.
- Create a username and a separate email ID in the crypto space which is no way related to your real-world identity
- Filter the personal information you are giving out in the crypto space
- Encrypt the files or folders which store the private keys
- Use hardware wallets (wherever and whenever you can)
- Don't store the majority of your crypto coins in cryptocurrency exchanges.
- Don't trust anyone and everyone

This chapter will have helped you understand the pros and cons in 'hodling' cryptocurrency. Try following the safety measures to reduce the major risk factors you may come across while holding a cryptocurrency and always invest only the amount you don't mind losing. The volatility in the value of the cryptocurrency can sometimes give a nasty shock just in case the crypto coins invested are more than the amount we can afford to lose.

Donating crypto coins or Bitcoins can be a much better option than holding on to the cryptocurrencies.

Chapter Three: Donating Cryptocurrencies

Most of the crypto investors or traders hold on to their cryptocurrencies during the worst financial situation in the share market (crypto-based) in the hope of gaining long-term monetary benefits. But unfortunately, it is so hard to resist the temptation of making good money when the price rates go high! Since the price of cryptocurrencies, especially Bitcoins, Ethereum, and Litecoins, have consistently shown unbelievable increases in their value during recent times, it would be hard to refuse to give in to the lure of liquidating a small portion of the crypto coins which are 'hodled' to get those instant 'attractive gains'. But this will trigger capital gains tax to the hodlers.

Since the IRS treats cryptocurrencies as a property, transactions with these cryptocurrencies are similar to buying and selling gold or shares or stocks that by default, attract tax as it is either considered as 'business income' or 'monetary gain.' Due to this recent tax enforcement on crypto enthusiasts, many of them are looking at our usual conventional method for reducing their 'tax payment.'

The typical solution would be – donating to a charitable organization or NGO. When you give crypto coins to an NGO who is in need of money for running their services, you get to save taxes on the crypto coins you want to sell. Since these are crypto coins' value is high compared to fiat currency value, the charity organization will benefit by getting a large donation, and you will also enjoy a huge tax deduction.

How does donating help?

Let us try to understand this concept with an example –

"You just sold some crypto coins which gave you around 1,000,000 dollars. After a tax deduction of 23,800 dollars, you would be left with only 76,200 dollars.

But when you donate these coins to an NGO or local charity trust, you are entitled to a charitable deduction of 1,000,000 dollars. Not only this, the local charitable trust or the NGO will gain 1,00,000 dollars tax-free allowing them to sell the coins without the need to pay tax as they are not subjected to income tax.

The charitable deduction for gifts of the valued property is limited to 30% of your adjusted gross income (AGI) which would help you to get a good percentage of gain when you are planning to sell the remaining coins."

The most significant thing that is to be considered is – "donate coins which have been held for at least a year." Donating coins that have been held for a shorter period might have very low deduction based on the value. Don't wait until the year-end to make that donation as most of the NGOs have a set of procedures to be done and you don't want to be caught in the year-end financial brawl.

Greenpeace, Red Cross, Save the Children, etc. have already increased their donor base through cryptocurrency donations (Bitcoin to be specific). The popularity of Bitcoins among the charity organizations is high, and it cannot be denied that the spectacular increase of 140% on the price of cryptocurrency since the beginning of 2017 has created this interest among the NGOs and charitable trusts.

Role of blockchain technology and Bitcoin in charities

The revolutionary technology which allows every participant in the network to keep track of the transactions made in a distributed central ledger and also maintain the transaction details in every single node instead of being controlled by a third party authority has created 'ripples' in the digital market for quite some years now. This technology known as blockchain technology, which is the crucial part in all the cryptocurrency transaction, is said to have a good impact on NGOs and charitable trusts too.

- Because of the transparency in this technology, the donor will be able to get the complete details of his transactions that ensures that the donation has actually reached the right place (and isn't misused).
- This radical transparency will increase the trust in the charitable organizations and philanthropy can get transformed into a new dimension altogether.
- When charities start implementing blockchain technology into their record keeping area, it will help in streamlining regulations.
- The need of maintaining separate registers for each charity made by a particular organization, entity or person can be avoided as when the transactions are block-chained, and you finally get real-time information with greater transparency.

Donor-advised fund

Donor-advised fund or DAF is a philanthropic medium that has been set up mainly for public charity. It helps the donors obtain an immediate tax deduction or tax benefits that can propose funding over a period of time whenever a donation or contribution is made towards the NGO or public charity. Donor-advised funds are the easiest way to deal with tax while contributing to the charity. They are fast growing in the United States, as donors find it easy to gain tax benefits with their charitable contributions. It has been eighty years since this charitable vehicle was introduced.

How does this work?

To make it simple – Donor-advised funds help a person to make philanthropic gifts and gain tax benefits at the same time. You experience joy by making others happy. So how does this whole thing work?

You deposit an amount you would want to donate to your donor-advised funds for which you will be receiving a tax deduction for the entire contribution made during that calendar year. Allocations can then be made from your donor-advised funds to the respective non-profitable organizations or charitable trust over the course of time as per your choice. The most crucial thing that needs to be kept in mind is - the money in your donor-advised fund account can only be used for charitable purposes. You will not be able to use the money to buy tickets for concerts or events arranged for the respective non-profitable organizations or philanthropic trusts, i.e. If a particular NGO you had chosen is organizing for a music concert to use the fund proceeds from the event of its organization's services, you still cannot use the money you have allocated to your DAF account to buy the ticket, though the payment of the ticket would be going to the NGO.

Advantages of DAF

- You are eligible for the tax benefits when you put your money into the donor-advised fund and not by just allocating the funds to the respective charities. This is when you receive a tax deduction for your entire contributed amount for that particular calendar year.
- Since a good amount of money is set aside for philanthropic activity, you will get accustomed to the routine of contributing to the respective NGOs every year without fail. Moreover, you cannot do anything else with the money apart from donating.
- This can be considered as a form of investment as the money you had invested in the donor-advised fund will keep growing over the year and is entirely tax-free.
- The donor-advised fund also allows the donor to donate assets apart from cash. Instead of selling a stock or share when the value dips down, you can donate the asset to the DAF making it tax-free because when you sell stocks or shares, you automatically attract tax (capital gain taxes). But when you contribute such stocks or shares, you gain a tax deduction of the full market value of the securities from taxes for that calendar year.

How does donor-advised fund with Bitcoin work?

To avoid the burden of taxes for the cryptocurrency gains made, many investors are turning to donor-advised funds. By now, all of us will know that the value of cryptocurrency is highly volatile and keeps fluctuating as the price value of these crypto coins is wholly based on demand and supply. When cryptocoins are used to fund your DAF, it is considered as an 'asset' as the IRS has already termed cryptocurrency as personal property and not currency. Transferring the crypto coins and liquidating them without significant cost is possible once it is contributed to your donor-advised fund.

Rules to remember

It is true that you can gain tax benefits by contributing Bitcoins or other crypto coins to charitable trusts or non-profitable organizations, but it is essential to be aware of the following rules with regards to the same:

- 30% market value deduction of the adjusted gross income (AGI) is possible if your crypto coins are long-term capital assets (held on for more than a year). E.g. If you bought Bitcoins at 2000 dollars, had held them for more than a year and would like to donate them when the value is 4000 dollars, you will be eligible for a deduction up to 4000 dollars.
- A much smaller deduction will only be possible if your crypto coins are short-term capital assets (held on for less than a year). E.g. If you bought Bitcoins for 2000 dollars, held them for three months and the value had increased to 3000 dollars, the donation made to a charitable trust now would only give a deduction of 2000 dollar, whereas if the value had decreased to 1000 dollars after holding it for 3 months, then the deduction would be 1000 dollars.
- In case you had received crypto coins as payment for your work, the deduction will be based on the market value of the crypto coin on the date the payment was made. E.g. If you were paid 500 dollars for a piece of artwork and were planning to deposit the amount to the DAF the next day, but by then the value increased to 1000 dollars, you will still be eligible only for a deduction of 500 dollars (as that was the value when you received the payment).

It is advisable to check on all possible options before investing your crypto coins on the donor-advised fund account for charitable work to get better tax benefits.

Donating with Bitcoins or altcoins over fiat currencies

Donations to the non-profit organizations or charitable trusts have always been in the form of cash or items (food, clothes, etc.) for many years now. It is only in the last couple of years that donors have started donating in the form of assets, such as stocks, property shares, virtual currencies, etc. Is there an advantage when you choose to donate crypto coins over fiat currencies? Definitely yes!

- High tax benefits
- The blockchain technology, which the cryptocurrencies are built on, enable the donors to view the complete transaction flow of the donations made, the ways it has been used, etc. This, in fact, forces the charity organizations to be more transparent.

The United States witnessed more people donating Bitcoins during the recent hurricane 'Irma' which devastated Florida to a large extent. The Fidelity Charitable and Red Cross reported that donations made with Bitcoins had seen a considerable increase compared to the last couple of years.

How to accept Online Bitcoin Donations?

Many charitable organizations and individuals involved in charity work are looking at various options to accept Bitcoin donations. Apart from publishing the Bitcoin address in the NGO's website or the individual's visiting card, let us look at the other options available. Using the following sources can help in taking control of the 'donations received':

- QR Code
- Coinbase
- BitPay
- Coingate

-   BitAddress

QR Code

QR code can be generated for the NGO's Bitcoin address and posted on the website to control the incoming donations from the donors. This can also be done by using third party donation services but using the NGO's own Bitcoin address with QR code helps in gaining control of all the incoming donations.

Coinbase

Coinbase helps the charitable organizations to accept Bitcoin donations from their respective donor base. Platform account has to be created by the user, which needs to be followed by a merchant profile creation. Post that, 'the instant exchange feature' can be turned ON to convert the funds to USD. The donation button generator in the Coinbase can be added to any webpage.

Bitpay

Bitpay, the company which processes payments for merchants, enables users to add 'donation button' to their website or create a hosted donation page. The hosted donation page can help the charitable organizations to design their own template based on their NGO's services and portray their need in a better way. Both options – donation buttons and hosted donation page; can be added to any online platform within minutes of following their installation process.

Coingate

Few charity organizations or individuals will want to keep their donations in the form of Bitcoins for long and would prefer converting them to Euros or US dollars. Coingate allows this option with 1% conversion fee related to the respective platform. This conversion fee is looked at as a minor disadvantage.

BitAddress

BitAddress website, which allows creating a paper wallet, also provides the service of setting up a Bitcoin address. This ensures the funds to be sent directly to the Bitcoin address, which is not linked to any Internet-connected device. This helps in keeping the Bitcoins in a secure environment.

Donating your virtual currency not only helps the charitable organizations but also helps you to manage your tax more efficiently and reduce the tax burdens

Conclusion

We have come to the end of this book. I would like to take this opportunity to thank you once again for choosing this book - "Cryptocurrency: Donate Coins for Massive Gains." I sincerely hope this book was useful and helped you as a reader to understand the crypto world, the risks it holds and the reason to donate crypto coins to gain more benefits on financial perspective. This book will have given a detailed description to understand the pros and cons of holding cryptocurrencies or Bitcoins.

The book has covered the primary objective which is to give the readers an in-depth functional knowledge of cryptocurrency regulations, the ways these crypto transactions are regulated, how good it is to 'hodl' a crypto coin or Bitcoin, things which need to be taken care of while securing the cryptocurrencies and the tax benefits one can gain while donating Bitcoins or other crypto coins. The book also gives a quick overview on how tax is implemented on crypto transactions by different countries.

I sincerely hope this book was useful and has helped in answering most of the queries you had in mind. My best wishes to you for making the best out of the cryptocurrency market by choosing the right investment plan and planning on the tax benefits, which is beneficial for you in the long run.

Happy New Year!

Sources

https://www.forbes.com/sites/greatspeculations/2017/07/10/what-you-need-to-know-about-cryptocurrencies-and-taxes/#1a63c25c1a95

http://www.moneycontrol.com/news/business/markets/worried-about-tax-on-Bitcoin-heres-a-closer-look-at-cryptocurrency-taxation-outside-india-2467251.html

https://townhall.com/columnists/lindsaymarie/2017/12/29/brace-yourselves-cryptocurrency-investors-taxes-are-coming-n2428153

http://www.livemint.com/Money/4cciHKjOYRIRgoMmKi8ypI/You-have-to-pay-taxes-on-gains-from-Bitcoins.html

https://coinsutra.com/hodl-popular-cryptocurrency-terms/

https://www.inverse.com/article/38905-what-does-hodl-mean-the-Bitcoin-meme-causing-a-storm-on-reddit

https://hackernoon.com/just-one-more-reason-to-hodl-Bitcoin-8874da1adedb

https://www.forbes.com/sites/laurashin/2017/12/19/Bitcoin-and-taxes-if-not-hodling-consider-donating/#e39db0e341ec

https://www.businessinsider.in/Bitcoin-donations-to-a-16-billion-charitable-fund-are-soaring/articleshow/59365305.cms

https://www.cafonline.org/about-us/publications/blockchain

https://www.fidelitycharitable.org/giving-strategies/give/donor-advised.shtml

http://www.frugalwoods.com/2016/12/15/how-we-make-meaningful-and-tax-efficient-charitable-donations/

http://blog.reninc.com/Bitcoin

https://www.nytimes.com/2017/11/06/business/Bitcoin-charity-donations.html

https://www.cnbc.com/2017/12/07/donating-Bitcoin-can-have-big-tax-advantages.html

https://themerkle.com/top-5-ways-to-accept-online-Bitcoin-donations/

https://www.investing.com/analysis/Bitcoin-hodl-or-gtho-now-200275704

https://hackernoon.com/holding-cryptocurrency-the-real-risks-3c54ca8d73b6

https://news.Bitcoin.com/Bitcoin-beginners-safeguard-cryptocurrency-holdings/

www.ingramcontent.com/pod-product-compliance
Lightning Source LLC
Chambersburg PA
CBHW070934220526
45468CB00005B/1763